SELECTED POEMS

Selected Poems

Ralph Gustafson

WITH AN INTRODUCTION BY
Bruce Whiteman

Véhicule Press

Published with the assistance of The Canada Council for the Arts,
the Book Publishing Industry Development Program of the
Department of Canadian Heritage, and the
Société de développement des entreprise culturelles
du Québec (SODEC).

Véhicule Press appreciates the collaboration of Betty Gustafson,
and all the publishers of Ralph Gustafson's poems.
Without their co-operation this book would not be possible.
Please see credits on page 85.

Cover design: J.W. Stewart
Fragments from Ralph Gustafson's manuscripts on cover,
courtesy of Dermot McCarthy.
Cover photo: Claude Poulin, North Hatley, Quebec, 1992
Frontispiece photo: Photographer unknown, circa 1943,
courtesy Betty Gustafson
Special assistance: Vicki Marcok
and Dermot McCarthy
Set in Adobe Minion by Simon Garamond
Printed by AGMV-Marquis Inc.

CANADIAN CATALOGUING IN PUBLICATION DATA

Gustafson, Ralph, 1909-1995
Selected poems / Ralph Gustafson — Montréal : Véhicule Press, 2001.
Poems.
ISBN 1-55065-149-8
I. Title.
PS8513 U7 A6 2001   C811'.54

Véhicule Press
www.vehiculepress.com

Distributed by General Distribution Services

Printed in Canada on alkaline paper.

For my parents
Carl Otto Gustafson
Gertrude Ella Barker Gustafson

Contents

I must be aging. I hardly know, or want to know, what I have selected. One gets ingrained with the dust of dismissive years.

So many poems I might have with justice included but for the neglectful attendance.

Which all above has nothing to do with the intention here. Justification I dislike as anyone who has heart on what he has chosen to do—the plumber who makes things work, a kneader of necessary bread, a poet and his musical language and meaning.

My intention was that I meant to delight.

R.G.
North Hatley, 1995

Introduction

When Ralph Gustafson died in the spring of 1995 he left two completed manuscripts behind: a collection of new poems and a new version of his selected poems. The new poems were published in 1996 as *Visions Fugitive*. This new selected represents Ralph's final thoughts on his work as a whole, even including pieces from the posthumous *Visions*. It is not a radical re-envisioning of his *oeuvre*, but clearly it brings together the poems from over half a century of writing that he thought most perfect and imperishable.

Ralph knew that his work was good, that it was part of the small body of Canadian poetry that would last, even if his faith in the audience sometimes faltered. When he made the current selection he had not published a selected poems since the early 1980s, and it seems all too probable that he wanted to make a final accounting of what he thought best among his many books—not a self-inscribed epitaph so much as a poetic letter to his readers and to whatever inconstant deity it is that watches dry-eyed over the reputations of poets.

Ralph's *Collected Poems* were published in three volumes by Sono Nis Press between 1987 and 1994. Before that there had been three earlier versions of a selected: in 1972 (chosen by the poet), in 1983 (chosen by Don Coles and issued as *The Moment Is All*), and in 1984 (chosen by John Walsh and published in the United States as *At the Ocean's Verge*). All of these books follow a more or less straight chronological order, unlike this new version which attends to a different procession of Ralph's own devising, choosing now an early poem, now a recent one, with connections drawn at levels beyond the order of composition: connections of theme, of music, and of private circumstance. If this version of Ralph's selected is not the one best suited to a reader who wants to follow the poet's growth and development, it is certainly the one constructed most like a typical collection, with affinity and devotion the force looking out over the greater whole.

Ralph's concerns as a poet are immensely various, but certain obsessions prevail: music, travel, the importance of poetry itself, his love for his wife Betty, and a hunger deeply to understand how the world and the cosmos work. Early on he records "the warring heart's huge anger," and even his most elliptical maunderings and his most elusive parings-down of history and culture are rarely articulated very far from a concern with "the valves of the heart" (which "are pesky things / And shut down"). He remains an allusive poet to the end, a poet who sees no essential difference between the experience of a canto by Ezra Pound and a flower in his North Hatley garden, or among an impromptu by Chopin, a novel by Trollope, and the grosbeak in his backyard fighting for food as the snow descends. The allusiveness in the earlier poetry can sometimes be difficult because it coexists with a highly formal sense of language and an austerity of music:

> Go tell the lips of lovers kiss a skull;
> The loin athletic, fathers dust!
> The great earth turns. The heavens move.
> Orion bends his bow.

> Mighty night and firmament of glory
> Here, on the yes of an eyelid hung!
> The broad hills break whereon you stand,
> Man of god who gave.

But Ralph's tonal range kept expanding as he aged, and in conjunction the necessity for formality waned. The result is that later collections are replete with poems that, however consummate their assumption of *Kulturgeschichte*, still sing:

> Aphrodite's laugh was certain
> (These are reliable reports),
> Not too loud; derisive, but lovely.

Ralph's publishing history was an unusual one. He published two books in the 1930s which he later regretted, followed by two limited editions which were incorporated into his first solid collection, *Flight Into Darkness* (1944). That book was published when Ralph was thirty-five years old, but although it was well received he seemed to go silent thereafter for over fifteen years. He was still writing a great deal in the period from 1945-60, but much of that writing was prose: short stories (collected and published much later), music criticism and record liner notes, and a novel which remains unpublished. It was also during that decade and a half that Ralph came into his own as a poet, with the result that his next two books, when they came out in quick succession, represented a new beginning for him. From 1960, when *Rivers Among Rocks* and *Rocky Mountain Poems* were published, Ralph really took off as a poet. Every collection issued between then and his death in 1995 shows an increased mastery. Perhaps it is true, as he wrote in *Configurations at Midnight*, his poetic autobiography, that "Endurance only matters"; but he did more than endure, and some of the most accomplished of his poems were composed in his old age.

"My intention was that I meant to delight." How many twentieth-century poets would conclude a preface to their final book with those words? Educated readers will think, well, certainly, that is one of the two central thrusts of poetry in the western tradition: that it should give pleasure and that it should instruct, following Horace's tenet in the *Ars poetica*. The Horatian model, although it became associated in the eighteenth century with a kind of conservatism with which Ralph would have had no truck, is not an inappropriate invocation for Ralph's poetry. The distinctions elaborated in the urban/rural contrast so common in his poems are significant, and no less the social conscience which allows for criticism but cannot be easily pigeon-holed as a Tory dismissal of the present over an idealized vision of the past.

Ralph was a true humanist in the sense that his aversion to postmodernism was based on a heart-felt disgust for the sort of politics that led to "a world of small boys with legs off." Ralph's political poems do not delight, because they focus emotionally on the horrors of the contemporary world; but he counters those horrors in the only possible way, by adhering to the delights of the microcosm. "Heaven is difficult," he says (perhaps ringing a variation on Aubrey Beardsley's "Beauty is difficult" which Pound quotes in *The Pisan Cantos*), but heaven for Ralph is always to be found in a person's backyard, lurking covertly in the physics of a drop of water falling on a leaf. He will talk about cosmology—he will even characterize his work as that of an astrophysicist crossed with a composer—but in the end he knew that theory could not hold a candle to the importance of immediate experience. That is where love (and heaven) resides in Ralph's most moving poems.

Bruce Whiteman
Los Angeles, October 2001

Excelling the Starry Splendour of This Night

Excelling the starry splendour of this night,
What link and lash that bind my bones
I think of now amazed whose hinge
Was even in seed articulate.

Or even on this sharp and dreadful edge
Of death my eyes lift up and see
Against the tug and tangent of
Our going, the centred stars.

Slow wheel the crackling heavens hung within
The pinpoint of an eye, my ear
Is sensible and whorls archaic
Music in its round.

Look how the architecture of this night
Is scarp and scaffold for an inch
Of breath and all its glory margined
By a breadth of palm!

Whereby what mortal crevice, coign of skull
Shall man be less, than all, this whole
And aggregate of god; snuff
With a pinch of logic, proof?

And he was fashioned in the sight of god,
That sits in conclave with his clock
Denial in his loins. He shall
This day surely plant turnips,

Fiddle with a shoestring: tomorrow serve
A grasp of gravel with his deeds.
O death, denied by every shoveller
Of dirt whose wage is love,

Come cranking, then, to him, test-tube, text,
Within your claw. No man that's sneezed
But will from all thy groans and gravings
Pluck the paradox!

Go tell the lips of lovers kiss a skull;
The loin athletic, fathers dust!
The great earth turns. The heavens move.
Orion bends his bow.

Mighty night and firmament of glory
Here, on the yes of an eyelid hung!
The broad hills break whereon you stand,
Man of god who gave.

Legend

Whoever is washed ashore at that place—
Many come there but thrust by so fierce a sun
The great cliffs cast no shadow, plunge a passage
Inland where foliage and whistling paradise-birds
Offer comfort—whoever has got up,
Standing, certainty under his adjusting heels
And height tugged by the tide, ocean rinsing
From flank and belly, ravelling loins with wet,
Whoever has stayed, solitary in those tropics,
The caverns of his chest asking acres,
                                        he,
Doomed in that landscape but among magnificence,
By shell and seafoam tampered with, his senses
As though by Circe, sorceress, used, exquisite—
He, that salt upon his time's tongue,
Knows, standing the margin ocean and sand,
Ilium toppled thunder his ears, what's left
Of Helen naked drag between his toes.

Biography

What time the wily robin tuggeth worm,
Dragging my grandsire from reluctant dust,
Did I, through fatal lips of unction thrust,
Lunge headmost lidded from Cassandra's womb:
Puberal, still with bended bow did shoot
Heroic arrows tipped at the fabulous sky,
Whose silver barbed the snow. To testify
The cryptic acorn plus the accurate root,
I, fool, with words of paper, scissors, paste,
Mailed awkward anagrams to Love and Death,
And lagged and loosed the ravelling threads that baste
This bone to cerements of flesh. Beneath
The purchase of my present jaw, I taste
The apple twixt the tombstones of my teeth.

Basque Lover

In the mountain-fastness lies
Nearer flesh than husbandries,
Fatal lover lipping mud
Pliant to his amorous mood.

On Cabuerniga's hill
Lavish death is conjugal—
Lover lying grasses wan
Almost as interjacent bone.

Egregious lust interrogates
The loins' forgotten postulates,
Curious passion scuttles down
The alleys where the eyes are gone.

Beneath the body's lewd embrace
Twists October's present grass;
And at the nostrils of the lover,
Quietly, the wind-seeds hover...

Spain, 1937

"S.S.R., Lost at Sea." -*The Times*

What heave of grapnels will resurrect the fabric
Of him, oceans drag, whereof he died,
Drowning sheer fathoms down, liquid to grab on—
Sucked by the liner, violence in her side?
Of no more sorrow than a mottled Grief
In marble. There fantastic in the murk,
Where saltwhite solitary forests leaf,
He swings; the dark anonymously works.
For who shall count the countless hands and limbs
In ditch and wall and wave, dead, dead
In Europe: touch with anguished name and claim
And actual tear, what must be generally said?
O let the heart's tough riggings salvage him,
Only whose lengths can grapple with these dead.

S.S. Athenia, September 3, 1939

State of Affairs

This is a world of small boys with legs off.
Hip. Hip. They walk the world grown up.
Bitterness is not unknown.

Of course always there have been legs off
In a manner of speaking, taking legs off
To stand for eyes out,

But that is expected—the previous century is barbaric,
Few honorary degrees were granted,
TV was unknown.

It is too bad since we have so many computers,
So many carbines and combines that we have
So many legs off

But it can't be helped, boys must hop as best
They can, bitterness or not, there must be legs off
So there can be progress,

That is to say democratic election,
Culture for the collectivity and less
In the future legs off.

The Newspaper

That photo of the little Jew in the cap,
Back to the gun held by the Nazi
With splay feet aware of the camera,
The little boy with his hands in the air,
I turn over. I don't want to see it.
As a member of the human race. I am
Civilized. I am happy. I flap the
Newspaper with the picture over
So that when it is picked up to be taken
Down cellar to be put with the trash
I won't see it. I am sensitive.
The little boy is dead. He went
Through death. The cap is his best one.
He has brown eyes. He does not
Understand. Putting your hands
Up in front of a carbine prevents
The bullet. He is with the others,
Some of them he knows, so
It is all right. I turn
The paper over, the picture face
Down.

Gamelan Music

Tranquility and sun, far away,
No matter the distance, the silver gong
Reverberating on the delicate air—
This immediacy.

The shore pounds, the incoming wave,
The tumult of the wave smashed in the sun.
I could wish, wish the heart
Calm as I hear the far distance,
The temple longing.

From one pagoda to the distant pagoda
Is a night's journey. No one, no one
Is able to make this journey. Far
Is the sun from where I think this,
Where this is.

The Certainty of Triumph

Spring moves and pallid under the leaves
The durance of winter. The thrust of pure
Rhythms urgent undoes the long year
And the sorrows and the snow and this late knowledge of death.
The wedge of iris breaks earth.

Sits a stone, he, weighted down with dreams,
Hears rhythms possible, grass and love, thinks
Green attainments into being, crosstree,
Resurrection, cockfriction. Fool!
Dots his i with diamond.

Letter to Akhenaten

You put the loveliest woman in Egypt
To take up with your brother. You thought
Love was all one and truth so potent
You could make it public. Nefertiti
Went to the North Palace and Smenkhara
The golden boy was surrogate for your own
Ugliness. Misfortune all round. The Window
Of Appearances at which you made everyone
Stand naked in truth before the populace,
Didn't work. The viewers were curious or shocked,
The truth wasn't what should be achieved.
Illusion was, the pun on habit clothed.
Not pot-bellies but rainbows and panoply.
You tried it with God, making Him one,
The one Aten, not cow-eared Hathor,
Horus the night-hawk and Khons with a boat
And moonshine. It was no good, monotheism.
The temple wants diversity, more money in it,
Your sundisk with its rays of little hands
Giving breath to the nostrils, your shining Light,
Wasn't enough though you move a city
Down the Nile. The old alleys are what
Men want, familiar establishment. You know
Where you stand then, not some
Abstract Benevolence up over the horizon
Somewhere. Cover your belly, go back to Thebes,
Give up believing your truth is my truth.
Truth is what is convenient and comfortable.
You can't win the world over with poetry.

Heaven is Difficult

       Unsponsored solitude—space
For a firmament interrupted
By a stubtoe agglomeration, stars!
Under whose aegis? Not a whisper
From anything but singing angels
Whipped up and stuffed in wishes
By fear of vacuums. Unfurnished tenancy
That or stained-glass trumpets blowing
A brassy fanfare from pointed windows?
Vasty cathedrals for themselves.

       Edifices and preparatory coughs
From eloquent pulpits about to speak
And solve conundrums?

                  I wrestle angels
Like Jacob sweating his surplice. Abstract
Premises or interruptive
Stardom, buttresses whose glooms
Hold fragilities of colour?

Final Disquisition According to the Giant Tube-worm

On the ocean floor, topped with blood-red plumes,
The giant tube-worm feeds. It feeds on water
Laden with hot sulphur. Crabs graze
The plumes. I suppose He created the tube-worm.
I doubt it. It has no free-will, it baffles
Evolution, it lacks martyrdom, it doesn't
Need light. It is undue.
                                    There
It ingests. Without plot of propagation.

Flowers for Easter

The cosmos a mathematical equation.
Yet sadness persists—all that striving
For the hereafter where nothing else will do.

Clouds are clouds. Faith, for the restless.

She walked the length of Wolfe Street
To the church to arrange flowers for the altar,
Logic no threat to Sunday, flowers
Reason to my mother, acceptable.
Design! The sadness persists.

    Suffering the means to get there.
    Adieu, forêts, Jeanne d'Arc's domain,
    Rough Peter's scriptural bait, the catch
    Considerable, Saint Matthew's tax collected.

Much is required for an adequate answer:
The cockroach is repulsive and the female
Produces three hundred, four hundred,
Offspring at a time. It hates light.
You may suspect that the life-force
Is not entirely related to Purpose,
The cockroach to Benevolence. Dichotomy
Infests the world. Some predict
The cockroach like the Biblical frog
And locust will take over the earth.
The scent of the dog, the reach of the giraffe
And the wings of the hummingbird, of these
There is no need of further praise.
I am halted by the cockroach and innocence.

      Keats and his steadfast star, Sterne
With his rage.

          Life subject to death.
I walk along this corner of field,
Easeless, aware of what has been achieved:
A jewelled egg, a belt buckle,
Versailles—hand to the new century
Immovable perfections, equations, AIDS,
Smokestacks to settle questions of faith.

      My father had an answer, a day
In a rowboat, in the sun, fishing,
Pipe lighted, moving the boat
Every once in a while with an oar
Into the shade where the fish are hungry.

      Conditional joy. That's about it.

The uses of detraction are a Bible
Diminished, the worm, that knotted in the soil
Thrives, that, buried, duplicates,
Limbless, eats dust. Izaak
Walton threaded one on the hook
Of his fish line, pulled out Eden.

Sessional Memoranda

1
First-flung small leaves,
Long days in the stretched-out sun,

The beauty and buildings of winter;
Shady meltings, crozier ferns,

Seasonal glory, these goings-on!
Love? That too, the two of them

Too close for communication!
All of nature spread out for inspection:

Summer's old ruins and habitation
Hunked to the side and good riddance,

Earthworms brutally threaded for glory
In weedy waters and cool patches,

On oaks old bark shed.
What do we want accomplished?

4
A long-nosed bat ears-deep
In a saguaro cactus flower, out
With a mouthful—

The whole blown desert accommodates life
Unlike the moon who's had it. Earth
In excelsus!

The roots of the banyan contemplate.
The suffering oyster donates its pearl.

Stars! Impudent earth! I sit
In awe, the sultry book of poems
Shut in my lap.

The Absurdity of Not Knowing

Colossal perpetration! Out of this,
Dead, not knowing the reason why
Of black holes stuck in heaven.
There they are, swallowing space
Beyond ingestion while we walk streets,
The universe up to something and Sophie
Buying shoes for sore feet.
Poor Sophie. Poor universe
Not having Sophie know why.
The Colossal swirl and mammoth pinpoint,
Children spinning tops, mankind
Screwing openings, birth to incontinency,
Dark about the eyes. Meanwhile
The true and starry heavens going
Somewhere with the reasons.
Redundancy! Infinity turning inside
Out while we eat prunes at breakfast.

It Is I Suppose Profoundly Sad

Inherent irony, yes, yet strategy,
Anger, cancellation—multiple
Stars above our head—a conquest
Of them—while we last—a thousand
City windows smashed, sun
Overhead. Imbalance. Yet
A pretty sight imposed, whatever
Landscape not meant to be.

    The North Cape up from Stockholm
Doubled back, exhilaration;
At the Hague the widower, the old man
Sitting by the water's edge
Content, knowing he had made it,
Love, he explained, the crowd going by
At noon. Underground in caves
At Kiev's monastery the heaps
Of skulls to balance the brain—
God loves that, the sleight
Of hand, the gradual offhand greeting,
The pain to get rid of this bone-house
We walk with, planned for.
The ambiguity of being born!
The bounced ball first-seen
To the last of the incipient moon.

    Chemistry? Purpose behind the infant
Heartbeat, the decadent old? ...

The Arrival of Wisdom

Of course the truth is there's no design,
Just process: which settles all-seeing God for good
And Him as a chemist mixing combinations
To get what he could declare without it,
Wanting to be worshipped, pitching beginnings
With a bang into teleological void.

Truth goes on solving nothing, gluons
And quarks combine, come apart, unmindful, stars
Go out, suns come on, the clutter ever
Expanding; sheep on the meadow chew, chew,
Man imposes until his heartstrings quibble
And breath departs lugging its baggage
Of unaccomplished dreams. What a celestial
Tautology to get there! fun in the dreaming,
Irony in choice, tragedy in the waste,
Getting nowhere with injustice.

Faith is an ignorance. Love without hurt
The only choice.

I should pray but my soul is stopt.
This is a bombast world: fig-trees,
Snow, macacos, ocean's hurl
And surf and surge, on applebough
As crag whose cave holds kraken or
With comb of coral mermaid cuddles.
All's mad majesty and squander,
And x and y or zodiac
Excreting wizard mathematics
Like a slew of ebbtide worms
Won't solve it. The sand is miles and packt
And moonlights wash the gnawings of
A million years. The globe cants so,
It's a miracle a man can walk it.
Listen to him: *I'll say my prayers*
And set mine eyes on kingdom come.
I'll jump the prickly hedge and scratch
Them in again. I'll. I'll
Not Hesperides, I warrant,
No matter what you will. Try
Scour this heaven-hung kettle of fish—
The sweep has greater satisfaction
Up a chimney cleaning soot
With good soap after. Oh, you'll hoist
And heft your stature by a hair—
No one but the Barber wiser.
    Hear how this ocean thurls and thunders!
    Crashing foams and ravels once
    Was muted marble Athens owned.

Agamemnon's Mask

Flattened, beaten out,
The mask of gold.
But an earlier king, they say,
Miscalled by Schliemann
Digging around, over-anxious,
His mind on windy Troy
And that return to Argos'
Scented bath—
Some Achaean king,
Loved, I suppose,
Who also had children,
Was important,
As the rest of us,
Eating the red bean,
Digesting the day,
Without legend,
Praying the gods,
Without much hope,
Then dying:
The gravesmith,
Out of love,
Beating the fine gold,
The drained face laid away,
Without much trouble,
Without complication,
Without much trouble to anyone.
No matter,
Let it be Agamemnon's.

In Dispraise of Great Happenings

Birdsong and the midge drinking needfully:
Otherwise happenings of summer afternoons.
Such great fountains tumble water
At d'Este. I at the spring unwanted
At the corner of the patio, my foot in it
Unobserved, pull weeds. The choice
Between weedy violet encroaching
Ground-phlox massed in May and red
And white and to be propagated, is Troy
Fallen or not, a thing of moment
And momentous choice whether the midge succeed
In swallowing smaller than itself or,
Should birdsong cease? Let Helen
Waddle down the street and be beautiful.
I shall go to bed far later on
And pull the sheet up over time.
Now I watch the cataclysmic gulp
By midges made and conjugate
What question lies in oriole song
Oblivious of Agamemnon and a thousand ships.

One Cannot Overcome the Nature of Happiness

Chestnuts roasted, snow falling,
To this day are loneliness.
No matter the crowd at 55th and
Sixth, the busy tapping their heels
At noon on the balustrade of the fountain,
The wind cold from the west, from the Hudson,
The charcoal brazier making bravely
Warm the southwest corner of the street,
No matter possessing love, chestnuts
In a paper bag, hard coals,
Pink steam at the corner of the city,
     a loneliness inextricable
Is in the awareness of heart that all
This glory is gone. Is it not so—
That what you love is its moment gone?
How could it be otherwise, this ambiguous
World: November, the pavement, Luigi
Old, his chestnuts eight for a dollar,
The snow falling, the street forever—
No escaping that wind from the Hudson?

Of Green Steps and Laundry

The man will put a large-headed nail
Shiny as silver into the green step,
Straightening winter's bias and spring thaw,
And the bird come obtrusively to the bough above,
His hammer will knock it crooked and it will have to be done
Again, and that will be important; and she
Will hang blue and white shirts and sheets
That smell of winter's cold on the laundry line
That runs from the kitchen verandah to the telephone pole,
And the pulley each time the line is launched will squeak,
And that will be important; and neither she
Nor the man pounding the clear air fixing
The slanted green step with another nail,
Will be aware of the importance, twenty
Years later thought of by him who drove
In nails and by her who saw to the laundry,
Who thought little of cardinals and clothespins who now,
Remembering, loves life, loves life.

How Still the Wholly Silent Day Is

How still the wholly silent day is,
Ingenious light never tired of.
The sun sets northerly, the last of summer
On the unchanging hills.

It is a holy hour given over wholly
To itself, no word proposed,
Remembering
Abated for an hour.

When last the sun went down there was quiet
As this hour is quiet
Summer's margin gone,
The sky uncertain now, uncertain.

Hyacinths with Brevity

You will use whatever watering can
You can, what knife to plant the bulbs.
I smell leaves and crab-apples
On the ground; the crabbed progression is under
Way, blossoms poured, jelly
In jars crimson in the sun along
The sill. That hardens it, you tell me.
 I shall have toast in the morning.
        But be quick.
The valves of the heart are pesky things
And shut down. We shall no more see
The like of these leaves again. They blow
Across the garden with this brief wind
That blows. So you will use what you can.
This trowel with last summer's caked
Dirt on the blade, and this can
And these forty bulbs which should be
Already in the ground so swift the wind
Blows and brief the constituency
Of sun. This piece of hose will do…
But you have the watering can…

Of Chopping Wood and Codas

They all end, woodfires and symphonies,
All of them, nothing is worse than each
Finished if you love music and are cold
By nature with not much on your bones;
Codas come to. Indignation
Flatters, but that is graveyard whistling.

        As you get on though,
        Humbleness is silly.

What I do is shape words
All night and get up late.
Chopping wood also fools
One. The Kaiser chopped cords of it...

September

The leaves fall like rain,
A light wind and they fall.
There is no stop.

No more the foliage of simple
Things, time's place
Within the heart.

Across the farther green
Where winter's hemlocks edge
The uphill road,

I keep looking. Wherever
I look, each certainty,
Leaves fall to rest.

At the Cliff's Edge

And so we come to this establishment,
With cows down the slope munching meadows—
To sit in the sun. Beneath the rockcliff,
Tide and ocean suck the caves;
Upward across the level, sheep
In heavenly safety graze, the rake
And noonhour leaned against the wall.

Druid, I braid the hanging stones.

On the Top of Milan Cathedral

Four thousand saints surround me.
My soul is utterly taken by the man
Selling Cokes from a red refrigerator
On the roof of Milan cathedral.

I am unused to this commercial society
And walk the lead slope near the balustrade
With mine eyes as if they did not see
The solid wooden booth and the counter

But it is no use: the sun broils
And the cathedral is a million dollar failure.
The Virgin Mary and Christ holding
Open like a miraculous cardiac his bleeding

Heart, are for sale in coloured plaster.
There are assorted bottlecaps
Amongst the sleeves of straws and paper.
I have sat among angels and pinnacles

Being hot and closed mine eyes to commerce.
The man's wife argues about money
But it is in a dialect beyond my comprehension.
I think of the indeterminate profit

Of martyrs and the shareholders in a better Company.
I shall unroll the end of a Verichrome
And feed it into my Kodak before
The host risen above me is substantial.

In Zanipolo: Venice

I turned around
unexpectantly
and yes, there
was a saint
in silk robes
laid out in a glass casket
with a sliding cloth over it
pulled back now
it being high holy
holidays
and a cube of something
disinfectant or
dry ice to keep
the face from giving up—
the hands being gloved
in pink embroidery
it didn't matter
if they rotted a bit

I took one look and started
not because the corpse
was there and I hadn't
expected anything
certainly not a preserved saint
at my elbow
as I was looking up
at the monumental walls
the only start I got
when I got over the propinquity
of death behind me

was how
religion
had managed
to last so long.

One Has to Pretend Something Is Amused

Death in a taxi going from here to there
Instead of staying put pursuing truth
In the kitchen or up in the attic or somewhere,
Perhaps making love or pulling up weeds
In the garden which is far safer and less trouble
Later on. However, one must be
In movement to sell goods and converse with the world.
Hazard is inevitable. Too bad if the heart
Gives out and the driver has to dispose
Of an unwanted corpse but he turned down the flag
On his meter and so must take a chance as well
On being responsible or not.

     On the whole it seems best not to make
A move. Though here again who can judge
When the kidneys and liver will shut down
Or in the statistically likely case I spoke of,
That of the arteries to the old pump? I wouldn't
Want to be alone in any case but probably
Will be, two loves and death
Never coinciding.

     A tip ready for old Charon poling
Your ghost across the river Styx would be
Appropriate. You know the Greek myth? Never
Mind. Take your earthly taxi to where
You are off to. Destiny will be as much amused,
Lack of understanding won't matter.

Impromptu: On Poetry

I planted Athena, owl, on the book
That wouldn't stay open, weighty enough
To hold down the pages—the owl
A paperweight done in enamelled
White, red, and yellow with two
Green eyes bought at a shop in the Plaka
Plato once walked by on his way
To listen to Socrates spout, the young
Men jumping around, their cocks
Bouncing which pleased the old man
Who had Hermes in his garden and hemlock
On his cupboard shelf... Wisdom
To hold down poetry (the thick book
Was poems). How sexy owls became
The emblem of Athena who isn't remains
Greek, it certainly was topheavy
When placed in conjunction with poetry which gets
Its purchase lower down on that
Which men die for, not her
Standing up there in the Parthenon
In greaves and helmet, clothed in the peplos
No doubt cotton like the hose
Worn by those brisk girls on bicycles
At Oxford...I retreat back down the hill
To the gymnasium where Plato picks
His teeth watching athletes...

                    The book
Just sprang back on its spine, *zap*
Athena's owl shot from its perch...

Desperate Saga

It is midnight. In bed,
The poem in shreds,
Brahms in my head
Making statements.

Turned on the rightside
It might work out,
Braincells knocked
To a new position?

I might then just
Have something
Life sustaining,
Like bread or buying

New shoes.
Perhaps turned
Back on my back?
This is not funny.

Impromptu: On Profusion

Not one but a ramble of flowers
Is necessary, a single bloom
Graces a shelf but when was Eden
Not a garden and Adam digging?
The nerves want profusion, a license
Of you know what, smell and blossom,
Worm and sunslap all over the place.
Not less than extravagance will do.
Perfection's parsimonious, only
The profligate flaw will do—to perfect
The poet in us. Jewels in the mud,
Nine symphonies and Haydn's you don't
Know how many which from which.
Moiseiwitsch put text in its place
Sprezzatura was what he was after,
Tempo rubato, missed notes
All over the place under the piano,
But what a recital, wot a recital!
Bach never stopped playing
Morning, noon and night on his organ
(Ahem…). God is in the profusion
Business, what with His push-ups
And prohibitions. Words, words,
Joyce was after; three floorsful
Picasso painted his fraudulent facts.
May there be not one
But a thousand boiled lobsters fresh
From the tank for the menus of hopeless lovers.

Ham the son of Noah laughed when born.
The work of the devil. One mourns surely,
Losing heaven, entering this vale of woe
And tears? I yelled so being born,
The wedding of my aunt six houses off
Halted. I knew the world—hung upside down
Slapped in the alien air.

                 Ham laughed:
The world washed away! Two and two
The vessel rode the waves, every body
Happy, snugly saved. Lion humped
The lamb, bug the bee. Joy went round,
The circle squared. Doves dropped in. Mrs
Noah complained. The vessel grounded, hefting
Pitchforks done. Ham begat Chaplin.
All was well.

        Sodom and Gomorrah dried, the lofty
        Karakorams rose, the Dead Sea
        Drained. Dignities of hood
        And gown appeared; solemnities
        Of font and pew. The rainbow shone.
        All was as it had always been,
        Billboards up, markets down,
        Pantries, ethnic enclaves, cleansed.
        Heaven hovered in purest style.

At the Castalian Spring

Reality is virtual; the soul, not-quite.

We sat beside Castalian waters
That year, at Delphi where olives sequester
Apollo the god of healing's oracle.
We sat, assorted tourists, together
On what was left of the marble steps.
Below, in the valley, the Crissean temple
Stumbled to ruin. The hot sun sang,
The crickets chirred, the guide expounded.
In the gallery to the side of us, the charioteer
Drove his horses to glorious war.
We were responsive. We heard how Pythia
On her tripod in the cleft of rock
Prophesied what was to come,
Her gibberish finely picked over.

Back to Athens, just
Acceptably polluted.
Next day to Egypt, proprietor
Of resplendent graves.

Madrid Midday

The hot Spanish sun was over the city,
The midday traffic circled the square.
My wife was taking my picture, the statue
Of Cervantes on the tablature behind me.
"Get off the grass!" the caretaker of the square
Yelled at me. "It's Don Quixote's! Vamos!"
We did. The superintendent continued clipping.
The snapshot came out but with little of the background
Perspective expected. Penetrable Gibralater
Was ahead. I had had enough of picadors,
Parrots and the corncob cathedral.
The caretaker was right. No delusion—
Windmills, eateries, global awards,
Ubiquitous software, celebrities and soap.

Exaltation

Thrust of impasse as if never planned for—
The Rocky Mountains across the harvest plains.

    The Chevrolet, hand-wound gramophone, records
Irrelevant books, piled in the back,
At the end of the driving day we faced
Heights, sunsets on the mountains,
Sunrise. Omission never thought of.

        We fed the deer at Wapta Falls,
        Sat by the open fire, pans,
        Coffee pot, done-with—ahead of us,
        Metaphors, glaciers, passes; across
        The vastness, solitude explained.

        We climbed Yoho, Revelstoke,
        Through fields of flowers,
        Our minds on uplands.
        Ability was initial,
        Poor-boxes, candle-ends,
        Forgotten.

The Trail Under Mount Michael

We struck a berry patch.
All thought of snow peaks left
With them;
Sweet strawberries.
In the mouth
They broke on the palate,
The wild juice,
Whose seeds are on the outside.
At the upper end of the lake
We washed them in glacial water.
All that day the sweet berries
Kept our heads to the ground.

In the Coast Range

Snowcrests were flung around us,
Fresh snow since last night,
Mountains dazzling in the sun,
The Skeena, wide here, below the dazzle,
Catching the shapes, the snow twice;
The railway along the edge, the road
To the ocean, the coast of timber and salmon
And wheat for Asia; the window of the coach,
The car corridor toward the south,
Toward the crests of snow, too low
If you were to stand, for them to be seen;
You knelt, you had to kneel if you were to have
The peaks, the actual grandeur
Above the reflection in the still water,
The river from the glaciers above.
You had to get down for that, kneel.
But that was the thing to do.

In the Yukon

In Europe, you can't move without going down into history.
Here, all is a beginning. I saw a salmon jump,
Again and again, against the current,
The timbered hills a background, wooded green
Unpushed through; the salmon jumped, silver.
This was news, was commerce, at the end of the summer
The leap for dying. Moose came down to the water edge
To drink and the salmon turned silver arcs.
At night, the northern lights played, great over country
Without tapestry and coronations, kings crowned
With weights of gold. They were green,
Green surcease and great grandeur, over the north
Going to what no man can hold hard in mind,
The dredge of that gravity, being without experience.

Heritage

The promise of the moment is what we had.
There, Appalachian hills,

The house, Lime Ridge where
The Junction was, the commercial road,

The covered bridge that was winter
Solved, summer over with,

Wisdom enough for coming seasons.
The years that generations served

Hostage to the harvest weather,
Mirror Lake the present token,

The crabapple latent, the fieldfence broken.
I stand again at the railway cutting,

Hammering fool's gold, iron pyrites!
And yet not so unwise, the heart's

Schooling. The attic. Under the gable
The albums closed and kept, boxes.

Tomorrows still assignable,
Yesterdays their own bequest.

Heritage! Trust returned-to,
The land, occasional, never left.

Quebec Winterscene

And the snow trodden round the yard,
Soiled with boots and fetched cordwood,
Straw ravelled near the barn—
The long snow of the fourfold land.
At dusk, acres clamped with cold,
Threshold and clearing everywhere white
To the distant scribble of alders, across
The frozen field snakefence
Like charred music; sky only harvest
Helps over, buckled with taste of tin
Dipper icy a man drinks gasping,
Sweat of warm barn-work a hazard
Once out, door-to, headed for house.

   At eight, night now pitch, the train,
Halted for mailsacks at the swung
Lantern—the far horizontals
A moment, a history happening
The hills—alongside, pants, monstrous,
Pistons poised.   Then pulls past.

At the cutting heard warning

        whose only
Answer is the local heart.

Wednesday at North Hatley

It snows on this place
And a gentleness obtains.
The garden fills with white,
Last summer's hedgerow
Bears a burden and birds
Are scarce. The grosbeak
Fights for seeds; the squirrel
Walks his slender wire.
There is a victory;
The heart endures, the house
Achieves its warmth and where
He needs to, man in woollen
Mitts, in muffler, without
A deathwish, northern, walks.
Except he stop at drifts
He cannot hear this snow,
The wind has fallen, and where
The lake awaits, the road
Is his. Softly the snow
Falls. Chance is against him.
But softly the snow falls.

April

The tilting of the earth continuing
Flowers will come up, the sun
Has been out now for nine hours.
New movements following runnels
Down slants between pebbles
Can be remarked by their sparkle;
Motion of air makes puddles
Known. Pale shoots, all
Month out of the sun, are ready;
The heart aches with the shortness of life.
Patches of soil appear and the lid
Of the bin lies off from the trash
Collector. The end of the violence of the world
Is awaited. Nations hold back.
Young men want their love enfolded;
Fern fronds are furled tight.
Watchers acknowledge the worth of worship.

Dirge for Gardens

The robin running around the new-mown
Lawn listening for worms, I worked hard for.
The skin at the fork of my thumb and forefinger's
Gone shoving the machine. I straighten a bent-over
Pansy, alert at the whistle in my ear.
Redstarts are about. A wasp goes into the hole
In the paper-grey cone stuck under the angle
Of the kitchen-door projection of the roof.
But they don't take advantage, birds and wasps.
It's the labour for the worm bothers me—'mown grass'
The psalms of David, the old testy monk, point out.
What's it for has a way of getting into the best
Of labour, though I suppose ambition is worthy of its abrasions.

The robin has given up pulling worms,
Putting labour doubly in question...

Hearing the Woodthrush in the Evening

Through the screen-door in the early night,
The song of the thrush. After sundown
He sings. I listen and the wonder is not
Of one song, wealth is about me,
The truth that even as the heart
Responds richness comes, such as
Music that is loved and heard again
Provides and love provides, no sooner
We turn from the lake where the moon is
Than the glory of a night without moonlight
Is remembered glorious with fallen stars
Reflected—nothing of our own making
(As being in love, sensitive for the moment,
Or in the compensation of a remorse
Or in the tyranny of other happening)
Grace of itself, renewed
The short phrase of the night thrush
All over again we can hardly take it.

There! again. In the falling night—
The passing song coming through
The kitchen-screen where I stand—
Repeated though I had not asked.

At the Rue de Buci One Evening

The evening was lovely, the dusk was lovely, the air
Was lovely. Again it was Paris—where they shortchange
Buyers and as a bonus are right. But lovely, the crowd,
The people, all of them, thievery elegantly done.
We ran into the noise on the left bank,
On the rue de Buci, music, spontaneous,
Natural, the best music, loved, the rhythm
Smart as heaven, nine of them, trumpet, cornet,
Trombone, two of each, one for the broadside
Tuba, the clarinet between. O
What a group sophisticated—eight of them
With him out front, bass drum, cymbal, pounded
Like crazy, punctual as fate the girl with the cornet
Zipping the clarinet's zipper at every break,
Gendarmes shouting to let the automobile through.
O it was glory, independence, impregnable joy!

Five Transparencies

TAO IN NORTH HATLEY

Picking red currants by the western hedge
I catch a glimpse of the silver lake
Every once in a while as I raise my body
To ease the muscles of my thighs and back.

The unknown bird sings and then stops.
I listen to the sudden silence,
Then begin picking red berries again,
Dropping them in the deep pan with the handle

Brought from the kitchen. Fingers of both hands
Are stained with the red juice, some
Of the berries are very ripe. I like
The stain. I am one with the bird again

And the quiet reminds me of that scholar, Tao Qian,
In his garden tending his fourth-century
Chrysanthemums, eighty-eight days
Out of the court and its weary obeisances.

Among these hedges and the red currant bush
In the corner, apart, listening to the bird
And picking berries, I too have a fundamental
Truth to tell if only the words could be found.

OF LU HONG THE SCHOLAR

For his learning and integrity Lu Hong
Received from Xuan Zong his emperor
One hundred pecks of rice
And fifty bolts of silk.

His thatched hut on Mount Song
Had a brook, a bridge to cross it,
And a glass house, not large,
To care for delicate seeds.

Ten views of Lu's hut
Are still to be seen with poems to go
With each view well apart
From the purlieus of the court.

III

THE STORY OF WANG WEI

More elaborate was Wang Wei's eighth-century villa,
Rambling houses, pavilions and galleries
Connected by bridges and paths (famed
Among architects)

Imposed neither isolation nor abnegation.
Wang was no happier but he had
Many perspectives to describe with ink and colour
On rice paper.

He commanded visual inspiration walking
His courts and gardens. He was wise
However. Dynasties of vast wealth
And pleasure foundered

On unrestrained expenditure. (By the third century
Gardens were already synonyms for extravagance.)
Wang walked his garden paths laughing
At the intricacies.

IV

THE OPINION OF JI CHENG

A better view even
Than you would have
Sitting in trees,
Says Ji Cheng the author
Of a treatise on gardens,
Is through the moon gate,
The far willow in it,
And across the lotus pond
Where the blossom
Unfolds from the mud
Unstained petals.
All this even in the midst
Of a marketplace!
Noise is shut out
When the gates are closed,
Notes Ji in his book *Yuan Ye*.

V

AT THE ORCHID PAVILION

Amid the harshness of pebbles
My reluctant feet wander,
At sundown I sit by the willow
Listening to the plucked lute.

Old Lady Seen Briefly at Patras

The stick firm, a short
Crosspiece on top, each side
The hands control the gift of earth
To walk back to her door.
Sixty years back she lay naked
To be loved, thighs the width of him.
But the walk is on cobbles,
Not too good at best, not
With bent spine and incontinence.

Aphrodite's laugh was certain
(These are reliable reports),
Not too loud; derisive, but lovely.

My Love Eats an Apple

She bites into the red skin
Of the white hard apple in bed
And there is joy in heaven
Like innocence and whitefalls
Of snow and waters dancing up
In among green trees perched with more
Apples in tight skin
Hard as a bite and containing
Seven-eighths applesap deadpan.
I try to distil this knowledgeable joy
In crunching heaven.
God sits up there amongst
His shamefully nude nudgers,
Praising sin,
The juice of the plucked
Happy apple
In great psalms and paeans
Dripping down His testamentary beard.

A Window, a Table, on the North

From blue to dusk and the lights came.
It was as simple as that
High over the city.
Not as a cry of birds, on wings,
The summer swift green below,
The situation was stone sober.
We were philosophers,
Saw over,
The world wide,
The avenues a distance of arcs
That enclosed like longitudes,
The single point of crossings
The polar night.
Ice came on in the park
A pink rink
And the band blew
Happily
The streets running forever
North and birds flew high
Companions to our honour
And all over dominion
Lights came out.

Of Cordwood and Carmen

Stacking wood to broadcast "Carmen."
Dumped in the driveway four runs
Of birch to keep in front of the hearthstone
Warmth, and her in the basement
Piling the future, gloves and purple tuque
And sweater on, disposition as ever
Not a hurt
Toward anyone's life. Arranging wood,
She hums off key to Bizet,
Love and that ace of spades
Which is death turned up.
Death, what hope for you!
Up through the floor I listen
To clunking cutwood birch for the fireplace;
Outside, a copper sun, branches black
Against the coming snow. Day
Sets and not many to count.
She hums.

Interlude

Breathing softly as I listened to Delius,
My love slept. The sun touched
The sofa pillow, orange beneath the window,
Her head below on the softness, one arm
Underneath her cheek, rounded apple colour,
And I thought of Adam's Eve,
He allover dirt trying to dig houseposts,
And of death,
One year her or myself alone. But now,
The sun, slanting westward,
Caught through the green glass bottle
On the sill of the small upper window
Where it was as she had placed it,
Death not right away
But near enough. I listened and
Delius' music of its own shortness,
Soft and passionate in its way,
Ended.

        She moves,

Hearing the silence…

              my heart again beats,

Watching where she lay

Hunter's Moon

The moon was gold and the leaves were gold.
The red leaves had fallen and the pallor
Of the soft aspen was lighted, as gold,
By the hunter's moon, the first full
Moon of October. She stood on the verandah
Facing that upper shining moon
(My arms lightly closed around her
As if the time would come now).
Foliage was fallen thickly, the lawn
Uncertain, the dry brown leaves
Fallen. Beside the pathway
The last flowers, a further frost
Was promised.

        She did not like the deer
To be in the forested hills. It is a hunter's
Moon, she said. But it was beautiful,
The moment, the way it was,
The moment.

We Watch the Blue-footed Booby

Safe at home, her beside me! Hours
Still to go until she is back, music
On the stereo, in the middle of the Mozart
The bellow of the cow not ours a half mile off
Full of milk and Uranus beaming facing
The rocketed telescope amid the unblinking stars.

Committees re-position commas. I wish
She was home, the doors unlocked all over the house.
It's winter. My heart aches—the logs burning,
Snow falling, happiness possible,
The salt oceans tumbling and so on ...

It is the gaiety she has, going off,
Her umbrella aslant, loving the thunder,
An unduckable challenge to calamities
Should they exist. She knows, of course
She knows, how sorrow when least wanted
Enters in, how shoes, eventually,
Get soaked, as a child she knew what's worse
Than indifference, love that demeans.
Everyone knows sorrows. A birthright.
She angles her umbrella sheltering
The world, wears her best shoes
In the rain—the ones in two colours,
Grey and green brought all
The way from Venice, the shop at the next
Corner just up from the Rialto bridge
Where Antonio did not know why
He was so sad. She does.
She has sordid sorrows cornered.

O I shall prove that the hatred
In the Middle East is curable.
I have turned on the footpath lantern

That works with the lamp on the verandah.
Three steps up
To the walk are well lighted.
It was to the post office she went.
To mail a birthday card.
The power of love is more
Than theory, she is back on the verandah,
We watch the blue-footed
Booby on TV
Dance. The bird reminds me
Of Joplin's piano-jig.

Have you seen the blue-footed booby dance—
One foot, the other, Joplin's ragtime rocked?
You must see that before you leave for heaven.
And the penguin in white-tie slide on his bottom
Ice down to the slippery sea for fish?
That too is worth interrupting
Adding and subtracting for. The prospect alone
Cancels any impulse to get it over with. Watching
The hummingbird confront a tipped scarlet
Trumpet will do this, a skyscraper
Going up, oil-patches watched.

Notice that the scales of drying fish
Wet in the sun, are iridescent;

That lack of stones deepens water,
The grain of wood sustains study.

It was as if I tasted cinnamon examining
The nature of mahogany.

Snow is a fit subject for logic.
The look of an equation is sufficient.

One could do worse than propound
The shaded moss-side of a boulder.

Within a building a light shines,
They work at night. No one talks.

Hamlet's shadows, Akhmatova's ghosts,
Old sorrows, what are old sorrows to me?
The arras is drawn, St. Petersburg survives.
What phantoms matter? Cassandra's loves,
Richard's princes in the Tower, the staircase
Silent? Niobe's weeping headstones,
Eurydice, Orpheus' broken lute? All
The ceaseless sorrows. Endurance only matters,
Mephistopheles' shrug and the plunge where
The last ruby sinks in the pond mossy
With forgetfulness. Let us sit and
Contemplate while horses' hoofs pound
Riderless across apocalyptic skies.
O vasty emptiness, sorrows of Lebanon,
Candelabra gutter above cloth of shrouds!

The Stars Settled

She opened the door wide to the verandah,
"Hello world! How are you doing?"
I've heard her say that a hundred times,
Each time the cosmos consolidates,
Stars settle and my heart grabs
Ahold. Everything works. Syria
Loves Israel, a short circuit
To the food freezer is nothing, the whole
Of winter hails spring, and frogs
Boom from moonlit trees. Yes.
"Hello world" and I am translated
And doomsday somebody else's concern.

Winter Solstice

I look at her in the yard,
She is removing snow from the entry,
She pauses smiling just
Long enough to raise
Her arm and point to the sky.
From my side of the window
I look where she points,
Above her and the shovel.
The sky is silver with a star in it.
The day is about done.
The winter solstice is
At 10:38 PM
I am told by those
Who know. She turns back.
The light is about gone,
I turn from the window.
This must not change.
This must not change.

Proposition for Gold Trumpets

Glittering with sun as the wind moved
Were all the leaves of the tree.
It was a concordance between heaven
And the earth. Below, evening fell,
No shadow, but a deepening green.
Birds came and went. The time
Seemed holy though there was no proof,
The leaves trembled in the sun and the tall
Green was standing from some force,
The birds sang for some reason.
It was clear something was at work,
Not only sensation. The man built
The new lattice-work under
His verandah and the sound of nails hammered
Was in the air. Five strokes
And the nail was in. Something was built.
You could hear that. An improvement.
On the upper leaves sun still trembled
Like gold, like beaten gold; though the air
Overhead was darkening, birds sang.

In the Back Garden

A good clutch of the hind legs
On the outer portion of the petal
And pushing inside for nectar,
That is the curriculum to follow.

I watched the bee do it, bees
Without a thought who work on instinct
Which brains curtail. I wish I had more
Of the genetic genius that allows it.

Brains can be beneficial, philosophy
Sorting out scrambling aesthetics.
But perhaps not. Not these days,
Soap and celebrity the uttermost.

I mention that young man of Nazareth
A pretty good carpenter by trade
Who put two wooden planks together.
Luckless though. I tell you what:

Brains and instinct both, each
In the right proportion: an open toasted
Hearth and carpet slippers for instinct,
Irreducible experience for brains.

33   *Life is earnest.*

Remark the wind. Winter was carved
In line and cornice-overhang,
As if Gislebertus were at it

Adorning Autun: devils gnawing
Jonah, a great crowfoot bloom
Overhead while the little finger

Of the angel touched Melchior
Awake, his arm outside the blanket—
Or is that Gaspar? Balthazar snores—

Sculpture on a capital—the three
Wise men, told of a star—
Their heads now kept in an ignorant casket

At bombed Cologne, frankincense
And myrrh redundant. Here
Most of the winter nothing bloomed,

The cardinal pecked for sunflower seeds
Under the snowdrifts. Degas going
Blind, the running colours failing.

39   *Comedy—that's the thing*

Saturday was the day of celebration,
The Golden Age, Saturn's, Lord
Of Liberation. Lovers came;

Thoroughbreds mounted; spuds sprouted;
Autocracy crumbled; sails went up
The river, majestic; pinwheels spouted.

Three achieved their poem, the others
Applauded. Everything came off.
Our Lady (a little tipsy) wondered

What it was really like, mirth
Compounded. Scheherazade gargled,
Jongleurs juggled. (No joke).

51   *Epiphanies are got to*

The instant when nothing need be explained,
Without need of challenge, the existence,
When the poem is; Cézanne,

Kandinsky withholding the stroke, the action
Of the stroke conceived; completion, the moment
Of arrival, the *Eroica* concluded, nothing

Desired nor renounced, the wanting of evil
Got through, suffering solved,
The bridge balanced, the structure, the inherence

That was in the raw stone, the temples
Of Paestum, the quarry the Parthenon,
The resting-point, Joyce his *yes.*

64   *The moment is all.*

And so the moment is all, neither
Desire nor repugnance except for the want
Of waste, the hurt assigned, another

His love denied, his difference decried—
Peace in the avenue of elms, autumn's
Turning, the ridge of the valley come

To the westering sun, the interim our
Design, insistence of our dream
To tell what was, what is to come,

Finally that which we do. Only
The praise of love, the humour gained,
The permanence of temporary gods.

Sources of Poems
(In order of appearance in the book)

Excelling the Starry Splendour of this Night
Flight into Darkness, Pantheon, 1944

Legend
Rivers Among Rocks, McClelland & Stewart Ltd., 1960

Biography
Flight into Darkness, Pantheon, 1944

Basque Love
Flight into Darkness, Pantheon, 1944

"S.S.R., Lost at Sea." -*The Times*
Flight into Darkness, Pantheon, 1944

State of Affairs
Directives of Autumn, McClelland & Stewart Ltd., 1984

The Newspaper
Corners in the Glass, McClelland & Stewart Ltd., 1977

Gamelan Music
Tracks in the Snow, Oolichan Books, 1994

The Certainty of Triumph
Fire on Stone, McClelland & Stewart Ltd., 1974

Letter to Akhenaten
Conflicts of Spring, McClelland & Stewart Ltd., 1981

Heaven is Difficult
Landscape with Rain, McClelland & Stewart Ltd., 1980

Final Disquistion According to the Giant Tube-Worm
Winter Prophecies, McClelland & Stewart Ltd., 1987

Flowers for Easter
Visions Fugitive, Véhicule Press, 1996

"Much is required for an adequate answer ..." (Author's revision)
Configurations at Midnight, ECW Press, 1992

Sessional Memoranda
Tracks in the Snow, Oolichan Books, 1994

The Absurdity of Not Knowing
Impromptus, Oolichan Books, 1984

It Is I Suppose Profoundly Sad
Visions Fugitive, Véhicule Press, 1996

The Arrival of Wisdom
Conflicts of Spring, McClelland & Stewart Ltd., 1981

At the Ocean's Verge
Rivers Among Rocks, McClelland & Stewart Ltd., 1960

Agamemnon's Mask
Ixion's Wheel, McClelland & Stewart Ltd., 1969

In Dispraise of Great Happenings
Corners in the Glass, McClelland & Stewart Ltd., 1977

One Cannot Overcome the Nature of Happiness
Winter Prophecies, McClelland & Stewart Ltd., 1987

Of Green Steps and Laundry
Corners in the Glass, McClelland & Stewart Ltd., 1977

How Still the Wholly Silent Day Is
Shadows in the Grass, McClelland & Stewart Ltd., 1991

Hyacinths with Brevity
Fire on Stone, McClelland & Stewart Ltd., 1974

Of Chopping Wood and Codas
Shadows in the Grass, McClelland & Stewart Ltd., 1991

September
Visions Fugitive, Véhicule Press, 1996

At the Cliff's Edge
Tracks in the Snow, Oolichan Books, 1994

On Top of Milan Cathedral
Sift in an Hourglass, McClelland & Stewart Ltd., 1966

In Zanipolo: Venice
The Celestial Corkscrew, Mosaic Press, 1989

One Has to Pretend Something Is Amused
Shadows in the Grass, M&S, 1991

Impromptu: On Poetry
Conflicts of Spring, McClelland & Stewart Ltd., 1981

The True Story of the Flood
Tracks in the Snow, Oolichan Books, 1994

Desperate Saga
Tracks in the Snow, Oolichan Books, 1994

Impromptu: On Profusion
Impromptus, Oolichan Books, 1984

At the Castalian Spring
Visions Fugitive, Véhicule Press, 1996

Madrid Midday
Visions Fugitive, Véhicule Press, 1996

Exaltation (Orig. "Impasse")
Visions Fugitive, Véhicule Press, 1996

The Trail Under Mount Michael
Rocky Mountain Poems, Klanak Press, 1960

In the Coast Range
Sequences, Black Moss Press, 1979

In the Yukon
Rocky Mountain Poems, Klanak Press, 1960

Heritage
Visions Fugitive, Véhicule Press, 1996

Quebec Winterscene
Rivers Among Rocks, McClelland & Stewart Ltd., 1960

Wednesday at North Hatley
Corners in the Glass, McClelland & Stewart Ltd., 1977

April
Landscape with Rain, McClelland & Stewart Ltd., 1980

Dirge for Gardens
Landscape with Rain, McClelland & Stewart Ltd., 1980

Hearing the Woodthrush in the Evening
Directives of Autumn, McClelland & Stewart Ltd., 1984

At the Rue de Buci One Evening
Tracks in the Snow, Oolichan Books, 1994

Five Transparencies
Directives of Autumn, McClelland & Stewart Ltd., 1984

Old Lady Seen Briefly at Patras
Ixion's Wheel, McClelland & Stewart Ltd., 1969

My Love Eats an Apple
Sift in an Hourglass, McClelland & Stewart Ltd., 1966

A Window, a Table, on the North
Rivers Among Rocks, McClelland & Stewart Ltd., 1960

Of Cordwood and Carmen
Corners in the Glass, McClelland & Stewart Ltd., 1977

Interlude
Shadows in the Grass, McClelland & Stewart Ltd., 1991

Hunter's Moon
Directives of Autumn, McClelland & Stewart Ltd., 1984

We Watch the Blue-Footed Booby (Untitled in original.)
Configurations at Midnight, ECW Press, 1992

The Stars Settled
Landscape with Rain, McClelland & Stewart Ltd., 1980

Winter Solstice
Tracks in the Snow, Oolichan Books, 1994

Proposition for Gold Trumpets
Sequences, Black Moss Press, 1979

In the Back Garden
Visions Fugitive, Véhicule Press, 1996

Gradations of Grandeur
Gradations of Grandeur, Sono Nis Press, 1982